THE FIRST
BLAST OF THE
TRUMPET AGAINST THE MONSTROUS
regiment of
women.

Veritas temporis filia.

1563

By Reverend John Knox

Lately modernized and prepared by
Joseph and Jami Weissman

Berith Press
P.O. Box 861, Kansas, OK 74347
(918) 896-2055
www.berithpress.com

The First Blast of the Trumpet Against the Monstrous Regiment of Women was first published in 1558. In this Berith Press reprint, in which spelling, grammar, and formatting changes have been made. All rights reserved. With thanks to David Jonescue, Logan West, and Alex Sarrouf of Project Puritas for their endeavors, and to EEBO-TCP for the corpus of texts it has produced. Printed in the U.S.A.

Image: John Knox reproving the ladies of Queen Mary's Court, engraved by William T. Roden; painting by A.E. Chalon, 1851

ISBN 978-1-963516-19-7

TABLE OF CONTENTS

The Preface...…...i
The First Blast To Awaken Degenerate Women……...…1
Summary of the Proposed Second Blast of the Trumpet..73
Appendix...……75

Scotorum primum Te Ecclesia CNOXE, docentem
Audiit. auspicus esta, reducta tuis.

THE KINGDOM APPERTAINS TO OUR GOD

WONDER is it that, amongst so many pregnant wits as the isle of Great Britain has produced, so many godly and zealous preachers as England did sometimes nourish, and amongst so many learned and men of grave judgment, as this day by Jezebel are exiled, none is found so stout of courage, so faithful to God, nor loving to their native country, that they dare admonish the inhabitants of that isle how abominable before God, is the empire or rule of a wicked woman – yea, of a traitoress and bastard; and what may a people or nation left destitute of a lawful head, do by the authority of God's Word in electing and appointing common rulers and magistrates.

That isle, alas, for the contempt and horrible abuse of God's mercies offered, and for the shameful revolting to Satan from Christ Jesus, and from his gospel ones professed, does justly merit to be left in the hands of their own counsel, and so to come to confusion and bondage of strangers.

But yet I fear that this universal negligence of such as sometimes were esteemed watchmen, shall rather aggravate our former ingratitude than excuse this our universal and ungodly silence in so weighty a matter.

We see our country set forth for a prey to foreign nations; we hear the blood of our brethren, the members of Christ Jesus most cruelly to be shed, and the monstrous empire of a cruel woman (the secret counsel of God excepted), we know to be the only occasion of all these miseries. And yet with silence we pass the time, as though the matter did not appertain to us at all.

But the contrary examples of the ancient prophets move me to doubt this fact of ours. For Israel universally declined from God by embracing idolatry under Jeroboam, in which they continued even unto the destruction of their commonwealth.[1] And Judah with Jerusalem both followed the vile superstition and open iniquity of Samaria.[2] Yet the prophets of God did not cease to admonish the one and the other – yea, even after that God had poured forth his plagues upon them.

For Jeremiah wrote to the captives in Babylon, and did correct their errors, plainly instructing those who did remain in the midst of that idolatrous nation.[3] Ezekiel – from the midst of his brethren prisoners in Chaldea – wrote down his vision to those who were in Jerusalem.[4] Sharply

---

[1] 1 Kings 12
[2] Ezekiel 16
[3] Jeremiah 29
[4] Ezekiel 7-9

rebuking their vices, he assured them that they should not escape the vengeance of God by reason of the abominations that they committed.

The same prophets – for comfort of the afflicted and chosen saints of God who lay hidden amongst the reprobate of that age (as commonly does the corn amongst the chaff) – did prophesy and before-speak [*foretell*] the changes of kingdoms, the punishments of tyrants, and the vengeance which God would execute upon the oppressors of his people.[5]

The same did Daniel and the rest of the prophets – each one in his season, by whose examples and by the plain precept which is given to Ezekiel, commanding him that he shall say to the wicked: "Thou shalt die the death."

We in this our miserable age are bound to admonish the world and the tyrants thereof, of their sudden destruction, to assure them, and to cry unto them – whether they list [*wish*] to hear it or not – that the blood of the saints, which by them is shed, continually cries and craves vengeance in the presence of the Lord of Hosts.[6]

Furthermore, it is our duty to open the truth revealed unto us, unto the ignorant and blind world, lest to our own condemnation we wish to wrap up and hide the talent committed to our charge.

---

[5] Isaiah 13, Jeremiah 46, Ezekiel 36
[6] Ezekiel 2, Revelation 6

I am assured that God has revealed to some in this age of ours that it is more than a monster in nature that a woman should reign and have empire above man. And yet with us all, there is such silence, as if God therewith were nothing offended.

The natural man – being an enemy to God – shall find, I know, many causes why no such doctrine ought to be published in these dangerous days of ours. [He will argue this in three ways]: Firstly, because it may seem to tend to sedition. Secondly, it will be dangerous – not only to the writer or publisher, but also to all such as shall read the writings, or favor this truth spoken. And lastly, it shall not amend the chief offenders, partly because it shall never come to their ears, and partly because they will not be admonished in such cases.

I answer: if any of these is a sufficient reason that a truth known shall be concealed, then the ancient prophets of God were very fools, who did not better provide for their own quietness than to hazard their lives for rebuking of vices, and for the opening of such crimes as were not known to the world. And Christ Jesus did injury to his apostles, commanding them to preach repentance and remission of sins in his name to every realm and nation. And Paul did not understand his own liberty, when he cried, "Woe be to me, if I preach not the evangel [*gospel*]."[7]

---

[7] 1 Corinthians 9

If fear, I say, of persecution, of slander, or of any inconvenience before named might have excused and discharged the servants of God from plainly rebuking the sins of the world, then each one of them would have had just cause to have ceased from his office [altogether]. For suddenly, their doctrine was accused by terms of sedition, of new learning, and of treason. Persecution and vehement trouble came swiftly upon the professors with the preachers. Kings, princes, and worldly rulers conspired against God and against his anointed Christ Jesus.[8]

But what – did any of these move the prophets and apostles to faint in their vocation? No. But by the resistance which the devil made to them via his supports, were they the more inflamed to publish the truth revealed unto them, and to witness with their blood that grievous condemnation and God's heavy vengeance should follow the proud contempt of graces offered.

The fidelity, bold courage, and constancy of those that are passed before us, ought to provoke us to follow their footsteps, unless we look for another kingdom than Christ has promised to such as persevere in profession of his name to the end.

If any think that the empire of women is not of such importance that for the suppressing of the same, any man is bound to hazard his life, I answer that to suppress it, is in

---

[8] Psalm 2, Acts 4

the hand of God alone. But to utter the impiety and abomination of the same, I say, it is the duty of every true messenger of God, to whom the truth is revealed in that behalf. For the special duty of God's messengers is to preach repentance, to admonish the offenders of their offenses, and to say to the wicked: "Thou shalt die the death, except thou repent."

This, I trust, will no man deny to be the proper office of all God's messengers: to preach (as I have said) repentance and remission of sins. But neither can be done, except the conscience of the offenders is accused and convicted of transgression. For how shall any man repent, not knowing wherein he has offended? And where no repentance is found, there can be no entry to grace. And therefore I say that of necessity it is that this monstriferous empire of women (which amongst all enormities that this day do abound upon the face of the whole earth, is most detestable and damnable), should be openly revealed and plainly declared to the world, to the end that some may repent and be saved. And thus far to the first sort.

To such as think that it will be long before such doctrine will come to the ears of the chief offenders, I answer that the verity of God is of that nature that at one time or another, it will purchase to itself an audience. It is an odor and smell that cannot be suppressed – yea, it is a trumpet that will sound in spite of the adversary. It will compel the very enemies to their own confusion, to testify and bear witness of it.

For I find that the prophecy and preaching of Elisha was declared in the hall of the king of Syria by the servants and flatterers of the same wicked king, making mention that Elisha declared to the king of Israel whatsoever the said king of Syria spoke in his most secret chamber.[9] And the wondrous works of Jesus Christ were notified to Herod, not in any great praise or commendation of his doctrine, but rather to signify that Christ called that tyrant *a fox*, and that he did no more regard his authority than did John the Baptist, whom Herod before had beheaded for the liberty of his tongue.

But whether the bearers of the rumors and tidings were favorers of Christ or flatterers of the tyrant, certain it is that the same – as well of Christ's doctrine as of his works – came to the ears of Herod. Even so may the sound of our weak trumpet by the support of some wind (should it blow from the south or blow from the north is no matter) come to the ears of the chief offenders.[10]

But whether it does or not, yet dare we not cease to blow as God will give strength.[11] For we are debtors to more than to princes, to wit, to the multitude of our brethren, of whom, no doubt a great number have

---

[9] 2 Kings 6
[10] Matthew 14
[11] Romans 1

heretofore offended by error and ignorance, giving their suffragies [*assistance*], consent, and help to establish women in their kingdoms and empires – not understanding how abominable, odious, and detestable is all such usurped authority in the presence of God. And therefore must the truth be plainly spoken, [so] that the simple and rude multitude may be admonished.

And as concerning the danger which may hereof insue, I am not altogether so brutish and insensible, but that I have laid my account what the finishing of the work may cost me for my own part.

First, I am not ignorant how difficult and dangerous it is to speak against a common error, especially when the ambitious minds of men and women are called to the obedience of God's simple commandment. For whatever antiquity has received, appears lawful and godly to the most part of men.

And secondarily, I look to have my adversaries not only of the ignorant multitude, but also of the wise, politic, and quiet spirits of this world, so that as well shall such as ought to maintain the truth and verity of God become enemies to me in this case, as shall the princes and ambitious persons who, in order to maintain their unjust tyranny, do always study to suppress the same.

And thus I am most certainly persuaded that my labor shall not escape the reprehension of many. But because I remember that accounts of the talents received must be made to him who neither respects the multitude, nor yet approves the wisdom, policy, peace, nor antiquity, concluding or determining anything against his eternal will revealed to us in his most blessed word, I am compelled to cover my eyes and shut up my ears, that I neither see the multitude that shall withstand me in this matter, nor that I shall hear the opprobrium, nor consider the dangers which I may incur for uttering the same. I shall be called foolish, curious, despiteful, and a sower of sedition, and one day perchance (although now I be nameless) I may be attainted [*condemned*] of treason.

But seeing that impossible it is, but that either I shall offend God, daily calling to my conscience, that I ought to manifest the verity known, or else that I shall displease the world for doing the same, I have determined to obey God, notwithstanding that the world shall rage thereat.

I know that the world offended (by God's permission) may kill the body, but God's majesty offended has power to punish body and soul forever. His majesty is offended when his precepts are contemned, and his threatenings esteemed to be of no effect. And amongst his manifold precepts given to his prophets, and amongst his threatenings, none is more vehement than is that which is pronounced to Ezekiel in these words:

"Son of man, I have appointed thee a watchman to the house of Israel, that thou shouldst hear from my mouth the word, and that thou mayest admonish them plainly, when I shall say to the wicked man: O wicked, thou shalt assuredly die. Then if thou shalt not speak, that thou mayest plainly admonish him, that he may leave his wicked way, the wicked man shall die in his iniquity, but his blood will I require of thy hand." But: "And if thou shalt plainly admonish the wicked man, and yet he shall not turn from his way, such a one shall die in his iniquity, but thou hast delivered thy soul."[12]

This precept, I say, with the threatening annexed, together with the rest, that is spoken in the same chapter, not to Ezekiel only, but to everyone whom God places as watchmen over his people and flock (and watchmen are they whose eyes he opens, and whose conscience he pricks to admonish the ungodly) compels me to utter my conscience in this matter, notwithstanding that the whole world should be offended with me for so doing.

If any wonder why I do conceal my name, let him be assured that the fear of corporal punishment is neither the only nor the chief cause.

My purpose is thrice to blow the trumpet in the same matter, if God so permit.

---

[12] Ezekiel 33

[In this way], I intend to do it without name, but at *the last blast*, to take the blame upon myself, that all others may be purged.

THE FIRST BLAST TO AWAKEN DEGENERATE WOMEN

O promote a woman to bear rule, superiority, dominion, or empire above any realm, nation, or city, is repugnant to nature, contumely to God, a thing most contrarious to his revealed will and approved ordinance, and finally, it is the subversion of good order, of all equity and justice.

In the probation of this proposition, I will not be so curious as to gather whatsoever may amplify, set forth, or decorate the same; but I am purposed, even as I have spoken my conscience in most plain and few words, so to stand content with a simple proof of every member, bringing in for my witness God's ordinance in nature, his plain will revealed in his Word, and the minds of such as are most ancient amongst godly writers.

And first, where I affirm the empire of a woman to be a thing repugnant to nature, I mean not only that God by the order of his creation has spoiled woman of authority and dominion, but also that man has seen, proven, and pronounced just causes why that it so should be. Man, I say – in many other cases blind – does in this behalf see very clearly. For the causes are so manifest that they cannot be hidden. For who can deny but it repugns to nature that the blind shall be appointed to lead and conduct such as do see? That the weak, the sick, and impotent persons shall nourish and keep the whole and strong, and finally, that the foolish, mad, and frenetic shall govern the discrete, and give counsel to such as be sober of mind? And such are all women, compared unto man in bearing authority. For their sight in civil regiment is but blindness, their strength weakness, their counsel foolishness, and judgment frenzy, if it is rightly considered.

I except such as God by singular privilege, and for certain causes known only to himself, has exempted from the common rank of women, and do speak of women as nature and experience do this day declare them. Nature, I say, paints them to be weak, frail, impatient, feeble and foolish; and experience has declared them to be unconstant, variable, cruel, and lacking the spirit of counsel and regiment. And these notable faults have men in all ages espied in that kind, for which not only they have removed women from rule and authority, but also some have thought that men subject to the counsel or empire of their wives were unworthy of all public office.

For thus writes Aristotle in Book 2 of his *Politics*: "What difference shall we put whether women bear authority, or the husbands who obey the empire of their wives are appointed to be magistrates? For what ensues in the one, must needs follow in the other, to wit: injustice, confusion, and disorder."

The same author further reasons that the policy or regiment of the Lacedemonians (who other ways amongst the Greeks were most excellent) was not worthy to be reputed nor accounted amongst the number of commonwealths that were well governed, because the magistrates and rulers of the same were to much given to please and obey their wives.

What would this writer (I pray you) have said to that realm or nation where a woman sits crowned in parliament amongst the midst of men? Oh, fearful and terrible are your judgments (O Lord), which you have abased man for his iniquity![13]

I am assuredly persuaded that if any of those men, who – illuminated only by the light of nature – did see and pronounce causes sufficient why women ought not to bear rule nor authority, should this day live and see a woman sitting in judgment, or riding from Parliament in the midst of men, having the royal crown upon her head, the sword and scepter borne before her, in sign that the administration of justice was in her power, then I am assuredly persuaded, I say, that such a sight should so astonish them that they should judge the whole world to be

---

[13] Read Isaiah 3

transformed into Amazons,[14] and that such a metamorphosis and change was made of all the men of that country, as poets do feign was made of the companions of Ulysses; or at least, that albeit the outward form of men remained, yet should they judge that their hearts were changed from the wisdom, understanding, and courage of men, to the foolish fondness and cowardice of women. Yea, they further should pronounce that where women reign or are in authority, that there must needs vanity be preferred to virtue, ambition, and pride to temperance and modesty, and finally, that avarice – the mother of all mischief – must needs devour equity and justice.

But lest we should seem to be of this opinion alone, let us hear what others have seen and decreed in this matter. In the rules of the law thus it is written: "Women are removed from all civil and public office, so that they neither may be judges, nor may they occupy the place of the magistrate, nor yet may they be speakers for others."[15]

The same is repeated in the third and in the sixteenth books of *The Digests*, where certain persons are forbidden *Ne pro aliis postulent*, that is, that they should neither be speakers nor advocates for others. And among the rest are women forbidden, and this cause is added: that they do not

---

[14] Amazons were monstrous women that could not abide the regiment of men, and therefore killed their husbands: read Iustine.

[15] Lib. 50 de regulis iuris

against shamefastness intermeddle themselves with the causes of others, neither yet that women presume to use the offices due to men.[16]

The law in the same place does further declare that a natural shamefastness ought to be in womankind, which most certainly she loses whenever she takes upon herself the office and estate of man. [For example], Calpurnia was evidently declared, who – having license to speak before the senate – at length became so impudent and importune, that by her babbling she troubled the whole assembly, and so gave occasion that this law was established.

In the first book of *The Digests*,[17] it is pronounced that the condition of the woman in many cases is worse than [that] of the man. As in jurisdiction (says the law), in receiving of cure and tuition, in adoption, in public accusation, in delation [*accusation*], in all popular action, and in motherly power, which she has not upon her own sons. The law further will not permit that the woman give anything to her husband, because it is against the nature of her kind, being the inferior member to presume to give anything to her head.

The law moreover further pronounces womankind to be most avaricious (which is a vice intolerable in those that should rule or minister justice). And Aristotle – as we

---

[16] Lib. 3 *De Postulatione*, Tit. 1
[17] De Statu hominum, Titul. 8

earlier touched upon – plainly affirms that wherever women bear dominion, then necessarily the people will be disordered, living and abounding in all intemperance, and given to pride, excess, and vanity. And finally in the end, that they must needs come to confusion and ruin.

Would to God the examples were not so manifest to the further declaration of the imperfections of women, of their natural weakness, and inordinate appetites. I might adduce histories proving that some women have died for sudden joy, some for impatience to have murdered themselves, some to have burned with such inordinate lust, that for the quenching of the same, they have betrayed to strangers their country and city, and some to have been so desirous of dominion, that for the obtaining the same, they have murdered the children of their own sons. Yea, and some have killed with cruelty their own husbands and children.[18]

But to me it is sufficient (because this part of nature is not my most sure foundation) to have proven that men illuminated only by the light of nature have seen and have determined that it is a thing most repugnant to nature that women rule and govern over men.

For those who will not permit a woman to have power over her own sons, will not permit her (I am assured) to

---

[18] Romilda the wife of Gisulphus betrayed to Cacanus the dukedom of [...] in Italy. Jane Queen of Naples hanged her husband. Athaliah [2 Chronicles 22], Hirene, Anton. Sabell.

have rule over a realm; and those who will neither suffer her to speak in defense of those that are accused, nor will admit her accusation intended against man, will not approve her, that she should sit in judgment crowned with the royal crown, usurping authority in the midst of men.

But now to the second part of nature, in which I include the revealed will and perfect ordinance of God, and against this part of nature. I say that it does manifestly repugn that any woman shall reign or bear dominion over man. For God – first by the order of his creation, and after by the curse and malediction pronounced against the woman, by the reason of her rebellion – has pronounced the contrary.

First, I say, that woman in her greatest perfection was made to serve and obey man, not to rule and command him, as Saint Paul reasons in these words: "Man is not of the woman but the woman of the man. And man was not created for the cause of the woman, but the woman for the cause of man, and therefore ought the woman to have a power upon her head (that is: a covering in sign of subjection)."[19]

From these words, it is plain that the apostle means that woman in her greatest perfection should have known that man was lord above her, and therefore that she should never have pretended any kind of superiority above him,

---

[19] 1 Corinthians 11

[any] more than do the angels above God the creator, or above Christ Jesus their head.

So I say that in her greatest perfection, woman was created to be subject to man. But after her fall and rebellion committed against God, there was put upon her a new necessity, and she was made subject to man by the irrevocable sentence of God, pronounced in these words: "I will greatly multiply thy sorrow and thy conception. With sorrow shalt thou bear thy children, and thy will shall be subject to thy man; and he shall bear dominion over thee."[20]

Hereby may such as are not altogether blinded plainly see that God, by his sentence, has dejected all woman from empire and dominion above man. For two punishments are laid upon her, to wit: a dolor, anguish, and pain, as often as ever she shall be a mother; and a subjection of herself, her appetites and will, to her husband and to his will.

From the former part of this malediction can neither art, nobility, policy, nor law made by man, deliver womankind, but whosoever attains to that honor to be mother, proves in experience the effect and strength of God's Word. But (alas) ignorance of God, ambition, and tyranny have studied to abolish and destroy the second parte of God's punishment. For women are lifted up to be heads over realms, and to rule above men at their pleasure and appetites.

---

[20] Genesis 3

But horrible is the vengeance which is prepared for the one and for the other, for the promoters and for the persons promoted, except they speedily repent. For they shall be dejected from the glory of the sons of God to the slavery of the devil, and to the torment that is prepared for all such, as do exalt themselves against God.

Against God can nothing be more manifest than that a woman shall be exalted to reign above man. For the contrary sentence has he pronounced in these words: "Thy will shall be subject to thy husband, and he shall bear dominion over thee."[21] As if God should say: "Forasmuch as thou hast abused thy former condition, and because thy free will has brought thyself and mankind into the bondage of Satan, I therefore will bring thee in bondage to man. For where before, thy obedience should have been voluntary, now it shall be by constraint and by necessity; and that because thou hast deceived thy man, thou shalt therefore be no longer mistress over thine own appetites, over thine own will nor desires. For in thee there is neither reason nor discretion, which be able to moderate thy affections, and therefore they shall be subject to the desire of thy man. He shall be lord and governor, not only over thy body, but even over thy appetites and will."

This sentence, I say, did God pronounce against Eve and her daughters, as the rest of the Scriptures evidently

---

[21] Genesis 3

witness. So that no woman can ever presume to reign above man, but the same she must necessarily do in spite of God, and in contempt of his punishment and malediction.

I am not ignorant that the most part of men do understand this malediction of the subjection of the wife to her husband, and of the dominion which he bears above her, but the Holy Spirit gives to us another interpretation of this place, taking from all women all kind of superiority, authority and power over man, speaking as follows by the mouth of Saint Paul: "I suffer not a woman to teach, neither yet to usurp authority above man."[22]

Here he names women in general, excepting none, affirming that she may usurp authority above no man. And that he speaks more plainly, in another place in these words: "Let women keep silence in the congregation, for it is not permitted to them to speak, but to be subject as the law says."[23]

These two testimonies of the Holy Spirit are sufficient to prove whatsoever we have affirmed before, and to repress the inordinate pride of women, as also to correct the foolishness of those that have studied to exalt women in authority above man against God, and against his sentence pronounced.

---

[22] 1 Timothy 2
[23] 1 Corinthians 14

But that the same two places of the apostle may the better be understood, it is to be noted that in the latter, which is written in 1 Corinthians 14, before the apostle had permitted that all persons should prophesy one after another, adding this reason: that all may learn and all may receive consolation. And lest that any might have judged, that amongst a rude multitude, and the plurality of speakers, many things little to purpose might have been affirmed, or else that some confusion might have risen, he adds: "the spirits of the prophets are subject to the prophets," as if he should say: "God shall always raise up some, to whom the verity shall be revealed, and unto such ye shall give place, albeit they sit in the lowest seats."

And thus the apostle would have prophesying an exercise to be free to the whole church, that everyone should communicate with the congregation what God had revealed to them, providing that it were orderly done. But from this general privilege, he secludes all women, saying: "Let women keep silence in the congregation."

And why, I pray you? Was it because that the apostle thought no woman to have any knowledge? No, he gives another reason, saying: "Let her be subject," as the law says. In these words is first to be noted that the apostle calls this former sentence pronounced against woman a law, that is, the immutable decree of God, who by his own voice has subjected her to one member of the congregation, that is to her husband, whereupon the Holy Spirit concludes that she may never rule nor bear empire above man.

For she that is made subject to one, may never be preferred to many, and that the Holy Spirit does manifestly express, saying: "I suffer not that woman usurp authority above man." He does not say, "I will not, that woman usurp authority above her husband," but he names man in general, taking from her all power and authority, to speak, to reason, to interpret, or to teach, but principally to rule or to judge in the assembly of men. So that woman – by the law of God, and by the interpretation of the Holy Spirit – is utterly forbidden to occupy the place of God in the offices aforesaid which he has assigned to man, whom he has appointed and ordained his lieutenant on earth, secluding from that honor and dignity all woman, as this short argument shall evidently declare:

> – The apostle takes power from all women to speak in the assembly.
>
> – Ergo he permits no woman to rule above man.

The former part is evident, whereupon does the conclusion of necessity follow. For he who takes from woman the least part of authority, dominion, or rule, will not permit unto her that which is greatest. But greater it is to reign above realms and nations, to publish and to make laws, and to command men of all estates, and finally to appoint judges and ministers, then to speak in the congregation. For her judgment, sentence, or opinion proposed in the congregation, may be judged by all, may be corrected by the learned, and reformed by the godly. But woman being promoted in sovereign authority, her laws must be obeyed, her opinion followed, and her tyranny maintained, supposing that it is expressly against God, and the prophet of the commonwealth, as to manifest experience does this day witness.

And therefore yet again, I repeat that which before I have affirmed, to wit: that *a woman promoted to sit in the seat of God, that is, to teach, to judge or to reign above man, is a monster in nature, contumely to God, and a thing most repugnant to his will and ordinance.* For he has deprived them – as before is proven – of speaking in the congregation, and has expressly forbidden them to usurp any kind of authority above man. How then will he suffer them to reign and have empire above realms and nations? He will never, I say, approve it, because it is a thing most repugnant to his perfect ordinance, as after shall be declared, and as the former Scriptures have plainly given testimony.

To this, to add anything would be superfluous, were it not that the world is almost now come to that blindness, that whatsoever pleases not the princes and the multitude, the same is rejected as doctrine newly forged, and is condemned for heresy. I have therefore thought good to recite the minds of some ancient writers in the same mater, to the end that such as altogether be not blinded by the devil, may consider and understand this my judgment to be no new interpretation of God's Scriptures, but to be the uniform consent of the most part of godly writers since the time of the apostles.

Tertullian in his book *Of Women's Apparel*, after that he has shown many causes why gorgeous apparel is abominable and odious in a woman, adds these words, speaking as it were to every woman by name: "Do you not know that you are Eve? The sentence of God lives and is effectual against this kind, and in this world of necessity it is, that the punishment also lives. You are the port and gate of the devil. You are the first transgressor of God's law. You did persuade and easily deceive him whom the devil dared not to assault. For your merit (that is for your death) it behooved the Son of God to suffer death, and does it yet abide in your mind to deck yourself above your skin coats?"

By these and many other grave sentences and quick interrogations did this godly writer labor to bring every woman in contemplation of herself, to the end that everyone deeply weighing, what sentence God had pronounced against the whole race and daughters of Eve, might not only learn daily to humble and subject themselves in the presence of God, but also that they should avoid and abhor whatsoever thing might exalt them or puff them up in pride, or that might be occasion that they should forget the curse and malediction of God.

And what, I pray you, is more able to cause woman to forget her own condition, then if she is lifted up in authority above man? It is a very difficult thing for a man (be he never so constant) promoted to honors, not to be tickled somewhat with pride (for the wind of vainglory easily carries up the dry dust of the earth). But as for woman, it is no more possible that she – being set aloft in authority above man – shall resist the motions of pride, than it is able to the weak reed, or to the turning weathercock, not to bow or turn at the vehemency of the unconstant wind.

And therefore the same writer expressly forbids all women to intermeddle with the office of man. For thus he writes in his book *On The Veiling of Virgins*: "It is not permitted to a woman to speak in the congregation, neither to teach, nor to baptize, nor to vindicate [*deliver*] unto herself any office of man."

The same he speaks yet more plainly in the preface of his sixth book written *Against Marcion*, where – he recounting certain monstrous things, which were to be seen at the sea called *Euxinum*, amongst the rest – he recites this as a great monster in nature: that women in those parts, were not tamed nor embased [*brought down*] by consideration of their own sex and kind; but that all shame laid apart, they made expenses upon weapons and learned the feats of war, having more pleasure to fight than to marry and be subject to man.

Thus far of Tertullian, whose words are so plain that they need no explanation. For he that takes from her all office appertaining to man, will not suffer her to reign above man; and he that judges it a monster in nature that a woman shall exercise weapons, must judge it to be a monster of monsters, that a woman shall be exalted above a whole realm and nation. Of the same mind is Origen, and several others. Yea even until the days of Augustine, whose sentences I omit to to avoid prolixity [*tedious verbosity*].

Augustine (*Against Faustus*, Book 22) proves that a woman ought to serve her husband as unto God, affirming that in nothing has woman equal power with man, saving that neither of both have power over their own bodies. By this he would plainly conclude that woman ought never to pretend nor thirst for that power and authority which is due to man.

For so he does explain himself in another place,[24] affirming that woman ought to be repressed and bridled betimes, if she aspires to any dominion, alleging that it is dangerous and perilous to suffer her to proceed, although it [should] be in temporal and corporal things. And thereto he adds these words: "God does not for a time, nor is there any

---

[24] *On The Trinity*, Book 12 Chapter 7

new thing in his sight and knowledge, meaning thereby, that what God has seen in one woman (as concerning dominion and bearing of authority) the same he sees in all. And what he has forbidden to one, the same he also forbids to all."

And this most evidently yet in another place he writes, moving this question: "How can woman be the image of God, seeing as she is subject to man, and has no authority, neither to teach, nor to be witness, nor to judge, much less to rule, or bear empire?"

These are the very words of Augustine, of which it is evident that this godly writer does not only agree with Tertullian before recited, but also with the former sentence of the law, which takes from woman not only all authority amongst men, but also every office appertaining to man.

To the question how she can be the image of God, he answers as follows: "Woman compared to other creatures is the image of God, for she bears dominion over them; but compared unto man, she may not be called the image of God, for she does not bear rule and lordship over man, but ought to obey him," etc.[25]

And how woman ought to obey man, he speaks yet more clearly in these words: "The woman shall be subject to man as unto Christ. For woman does not have her example from the body and from the flesh, that so she shall

---

[25] *On Continence*, chapter 4

be subject to man, as the flesh is unto the spirit. Because the flesh in the weakness and mortality of this life, lusts and strives against the Spirit, and therefore would not the Holy Ghost give example of subjection to the woman of any such thing," etc.

This sentence of Augustine ought to be noted of all women, for in it he plainly affirms that woman ought to be subject to man; that she never ought more to desire preeminence above him than that she ought to desire above Christ Jesus.

With Augustine agrees in every point St. Ambrose, who thus writes in his *Hexaemeron*: "Adam was deceived by Eve, and not Eve by Adam, and therefore just it is that woman receive and acknowledge him for governor whom she called to sin, lest that again she slide and fall by womanly facility."[26]

And writing upon the epistle to the Ephesians, he says: "Let women be subject to their own husbands as unto the Lord; for the man is head to the woman, and Christ is head to the congregation, and he is the Savior of the body; but the congregation is subject to Christ, even so ought women to be to their husbands in all things."

He proceeds further, saying that women are commanded to be subject to men by the law of nature, because man is the author or beginner of the woman, for as

---

[26] Book 5 Chapter 7

Christ is the head of the church, so is man of the woman. From Christ, the church took beginning, and therefore it is subject unto him; even so did woman take beginning from man, that she should be subject.

Thus we hear the agreeing of these two writers to be such, that a man might judge the one to have stolen the words and sentences from the other. And yet plain it is that during the time of their writing, the one was far distant from the other. But the Holy Ghost, who is the Spirit of concord and unity, did so illuminate their hearts, and direct their tongues and pens, that as they did conceive and understand one truth, so did they pronounce and utter the same, leaving a testimony of their knowledge and concord to us their posterity.

If any think that all these former sentences are spoken only of the subjection of the married woman to her husband, as before I have proved the contrary by the plain words and reasoning of St. Paul, so shall I shortly do the same, by other testimonies of the aforesaid writers. The same Ambrose writing upon the second chapter of the first epistle to Timothy, after he has spoken much of the simple arrayment of women, he adds these words: "Woman ought not only to have simple arrayment, but all authority is to be denied unto her, for she must be in subjection to man (of whom she has taken her original) as well in habit as in service." And after a few words, he says: "because death did enter into the world by her, there is no boldness that ought to be permitted unto her, but she ought to be in humility." Hereof it is plain that from all women – be she married or unmarried – is all authority taken to execute any office that appertains to man.

Yea, plain it is that all women are commanded to serve, and to be in humility and subjection. This thing yet speaks the same writer more plainly in these words: "It is not permitted to women to speak, but to be in silence, as the law says."[27] What does the law say? "Unto thy husband, shall thy conversion be, and he shall bear dominion over thee."

"This is a special law," says Ambrose, "whose sentence, lest it should be violated, infirmed, or made weak, women are commanded to be in silence." Here he includes all women. And yet he proceeds further in the same place saying: "It is [shameful] for them to presume to speak of the law in the house of the Lord, who has commanded them to be subject to their men." But most plainly, he speaks, writing upon Romans 16, upon these words: "Salute Rufus and his mother." "For this cause," says Ambrose, "did the apostle place Rufus before his mother, for the election of the administration of the grace of God, in which a woman has no place. For he was chosen and promoted by the Lord to take care over his business, that is, over the church, to

---

[27] Ambrose on 1 Corinthians 14; Genesis 3

which office could not his mother be appointed, albeit she was a woman so holy that the apostle called her his *mother*."[28]

Hereof it is plain that the administration of the grace of God is denied to all women. By *the administration of God's grace* is understood, not only the preaching of the Word and administration of the sacraments, by which the grace of God is presented and ordinarily distributed unto man, but also the administration of civil justice, by which, virtue ought to be maintained and vices punished – the execution whereof is no less denied to woman than is the preaching of the gospel, or administration of the sacraments, as hereafter shall most plainly appear.

Chrysostom – amongst the Greek writers, of no small credit – speaking in rebuke of men, who in his days, were become inferior to some women in wit and in godliness, says: "For this cause was woman put under your power (he speaks to man in general) and you were pronounced lord over her, that she should obey you, and that the head should not follow the feet. But often it is, that we see the contrary, that he who in his order ought to be the head, does not keep the order of the feet (that is, does not rule the feet) and that she that is in place of the foot, is constituted to be the head."[29]

---

[28] Whose house I pray you ought the parliament house to be: God's or the devil's?

[29] Chrysostom, Homily 17 on Genesis

He speaks these words, as it were, in admiration that man has become so brutish that he did not consider it to be a thing most monstrous that woman should be preferred to man in anything, whom God had subjected to man in all things. He proceeds saying: "Nevertheless, it is the part of the man with diligent care to repel the woman that gives him wicked counsel. And woman – who gave that pestilent counsel to man – ought at all times to have the punishment which was given to Eve sounding in her ears."[30]

And in another place he induces God speaking to the woman in this sort: "Because you left him, of whose nature you were a participant, and for whom you were formed, and you have had pleasure to have familiarity with that wicked beast, and would take his counsel, therefore I subject you to man, and I appoint and affirm him to be your lord, that you may acknowledge his dominion, and because you could not bear rule learn well to be ruled."[31]

Why they should not bear rule, he declares in other places, saying: "Womankind is imprudent and soft (or flexible): *imprudent* because she cannot consider with wisdom and reason the things which she hears and sees; and *soft* she is, because she is easily bowed."

I know that Chrysostom brings in these words to declare the cause why false prophets do commonly deceive

---

[30] Homily 15 on Genesis
[31] [May] God grant all women hearts to understand and follow this sentence.

women, because they are easily persuaded to any opinion, especially if it is against God, and because they lack prudence and right reason to judge the things that are spoken.[32] But hereof may their nature be espied, and the vices of the same, which in no way ought to be in those that are appointed to govern others. For they ought to be constant, stable, prudent, and doing everything with discretion and reason, which virtues women cannot have in equality with men.

For that he does witness in another place,[33] saying: "Women have in themselves a tickling and study of vainglory, and that they may have common with men. They are suddenly moved to anger, and that they have also common with some men. But virtues in which they excel, they have not common with man, and therefore has the apostle removed them from the office of teaching, which is an evident proof that in virtue they far differ from man."

Let the reasons of this writer be marked, for further he yet proceeds. After he has in many words lamented the effeminate manners of men, who were so far degenerate to the weakness of women, that some might have demanded: *Why may not women teach amongst such a sort of men, who in wisdom and godliness are become inferior unto women?*

---

[32] On Matthew 23, Homily 44
[33] On Ephesians 4, Sermon 13

He finally concludes that notwithstanding that men are degenerate, yet may not women usurp any authority above them, and in the end, he adds these words: "These things do not I speak to extol [women], but to the confusion and shame of ourselves, and to admonish us to take again the dominion that is meet and convenient for us, not only that power which is according to the excellency of dignity, but that which is according to providence, and according to help, and virtue. For then is the body in best proportion, when it has the best governor."

O that both man and woman should consider the profound counsel and admonition of this father! He would not that man for appetite of any vainglory should desire preeminence above woman.

For God has not made man to be head for any such cause, but having respect to that weakness and imperfection which always lets woman to govern. He has ordained man to be superior, and that means Chrysostom, saying: "Then is the body in best proportion, when it has the best governor. But woman can never be the best governor, by reason that she – being spoiled [*deprived*] of the spirit of regiment – can never attain to that degree to be called or judged a good governor. Because in the nature of all women lurks such vices, as in good governors are not tolerable."

This the same writer expresses in these words: "Womankind is rash and foolhardy, and their covetousness is like the gulf of hell, that is, insatiable."[34] And therefore in another place,[35] he will that woman shall have nothing to do in judgment, in common affairs, or in the regiment of the commonwealth, because she is impatient of troubles, but that she shall live in tranquility, and quietness. And if she has occasion to go from the house, that yet she shall have no matter of trouble, neither to follow her, nor to be offered unto her, as commonly there must be to such as bear authority.

And with Chrysostom fully agrees Basilius Magnus in a sermon which he makes upon some places of Scripture, wherein he reproves various vices, and amongst the rest, he affirms woman to be a tender creature, flexible, soft, and pitiful, which nature God has given unto her [so] that she may be apt to nourish children. This facility of the woman did Satan abuse, and thereby brought her from the obedience of God.

And therefore in various other places does he conclude that she is not apt to bear rule, and that she is forbidden to teach. Innumerable more testimonies of all sorts of writers may be adduced for the same purpose, but with these I stand content, judging it sufficient to stop the mouth of

---

[34] On Job 22, Homily 87 [or possibly *John*, although there is no John 22]

[35] On Job, Homily 41 [or possibly *John*]

such as accuse and condemn all doctrine as heretical, which displeases them in any point that I have proved, by the determinations and laws of men illuminated only by the light of nature, by the order of God's creation, by the curse and maledictions pronounced against woman, by the mouth of Saint Paul, who is the interpreter of God's sentence, and law, and finally, by the minds of those writers, who in the church of God, have been always held in greatest reverence, that it is a thing most repugnant to nature, to God's will and appointed ordinance (yea that it cannot be without contumely [*insult*] committed against God) that a woman should be promoted to dominion or empire to reign over man, be it in realm, nation, province or city.

Now it remains in a few words to be shown that the same empire of women is the subversion of good order equity and justice. Augustine defines *order* to be that thing by which God has appointed and ordained all things.[36] Note well, reader, that Augustine will admit no order where God's appointment is absent and lacking. And in another place,[37] he says that order is a disposition, giving their own proper places to things that are unequal, which he terms in Latin *parium et disparium*, that is: *of things equal or like*, and *things unequal or unlike*.

---

[36] *On Order*, Book 1 Chapter 10
[37] *The City of God*, Book 19 Chapter 13

- Of these two places and of the whole disputation which is contained in his second book of *On Order*, it is evident that whatsoever is done either without the assurance of God's will, or else against his will manifestly revealed in his Word, is done against order.
- But such is the empire and regiment of all woman (as evidently before is declared).
- And therefore, I say, it is a thing plainly repugnant to good order – yea, it is the subversion of the same.

If anyone wishes to reject the definition of Augustine as either not proper to this purpose, or else as insufficient to prove my intent, then let the same man understand that in so doing, he has not infirmed [*weakened*] my argument at all. For as I depend not upon the determinations of men, so think I my cause no weaker, albeit their authority be denied unto me, provided that God by his will revealed, and manifest word, stand plain and evident on my side.

That God has subjected womankind to man by the order of his creation, and by the curse that he has pronounced against her, is before declared. Besides these, he has set before our eyes, two other mirrors and glasses, in which he wills that we should behold the order, which he has appointed and established in nature. The one is the natural body of man; the other is the political or civil body of that commonwealth, in which God by his own Word has appointed an order.

In the natural body of man, God has appointed an order, [so] that the head shall occupy the uppermost place. And the head he has joined with the body, that from it, does life and motion flow to the rest of the members. In it has he placed the eye to see, the ear to hear, and the tongue to speak, which offices are appointed to none other member of the body. The rest of the members have everyone their own place and office appointed, but none may have neither the place nor office of the head. For who would not judge that body to be a monster where there was no head eminent above the rest, but that the eyes were in the hands, the tongue and mouth beneath in the belly, and the ears in the feet?

Men, I say, should not only pronounce this body to be a monster, but assuredly they might conclude that such a body could not long endure. And no less monstrous is the body of that commonwealth where a woman bears empire. For either does it lack a lawful head (as in very deed it does) or else there is an idol exalted in the place of the true head. An *idol* I call that which has the form and appearance, but lacks the virtue and strength, which the name and proportion do resemble and promise. As images have face, nose, eyes, mouth, hands and feet painted, but the use of the same cannot the craft and art of man give them, as the

Holy Ghost by the mouth of David teaches us, saying: "They have eyes, but they see not; mouth, but they speak not, nose, but they smell not, hands and feet, but they neither touch nor have power to go."[38] And such, I say, is every realm and nation where a woman bears dominion.

For in spite of God (he of his just judgment, so giving them over unto a reprobate mind) may a realm, I confess, exalt up a woman to that monstriferous honor, to be esteemed as head. But impossible it is to man and angel to give unto her the properties and perfect offices of a lawful head. For the same God that has denied power to the hand to speak, to the belly to hear, and to the feet to see, has denied to woman power to command man, and has taken away wisdom to consider, and providence to foresee the things, that be profitable to the commonwealth – yea, finally he has denied to her in any case to be head to man; but plainly has pronounced that man is head to woman, even as Christ is head to all man.[39]

If men in a blind rage should assemble together, and appoint themselves another head than Jesus Christ (as the papists have done their Romish Antichrist), [then] should Christ therefore lose his own dignity, or should God give to that counterfeit head power to give life to the body, to see whatsoever might damage or hurt it, to speak in

---

[38] Psalm 115
[39] 1 Corinthians 11

defense, and to hear the request of every subject? It is certain that he would not. For that honor he has appointed before all times to his only Son, and the same will he give to no creature besides; no more will he admit, nor accept woman to be the lawful head over man, although man, devil, and angel will conjure in their favor. For seeing as he has subjected her to one (as before is said), he will never permit her to reign over many. Seeing as he has commanded her to hear, and obey one, he will not suffer that she speak, and with usurped authority, command realms and nations.

Chrysostom – explaining these words of the apostle "The head of woman is man"[40] – compares God in his universal regiment to a king sitting in his royal majesty, to whom all his subjects commanded to give homage and obedience, appear before him, bearing everyone such a badge and cognizance of dignity and honor, as he has given to them, which if they despise and contemn, then do they dishonor their king.[41] "Even so," says he, "ought man and woman to appear before God, bearing the ensigns of the condition, which they have received of him".

"Man has received a certain glory and dignity above the woman, and therefore ought he to appear before his high majesty, bearing the sign of his honor, having no

---

[40] 1 Corinthians 11
[41] Mark the similitude of Chrysostom.

coverture upon his head, to witness that in earth man has no head;" (Beware, Chrysostom, what you say, you shall be reputed a traitor if English men hear you! For they must have my sovereign lady and mistress, and Scotland has drunk also the enchantment and venom of Circe. Let it be so to their own shame and confusion! He proceeds in these words): "But woman ought to be covered, to witness that on earth she has a head, that is man. True it is, woman is covered in both the said realms, but it is not with the sign of subjection, but it is with the sign of superiority, to wit: with the royal crown." To that he answers in these words: "What if man neglect his honor? He is no less to be mocked than if a king should depose himself of his diadem or crown and royal estate, and clothe himself in the habit of a slave."

What, I pray you, should this godly father have said, if he had seen all the men of a realm or nation fall down before a woman? If he had seen the crown, scepter, and sword, which are ensigns of the royal dignity, given to her, and a woman cursed of God, and made subject to man, placed in the throne of justice, to sit as God's lieutenant? What, I say, in this behalf, should any heart unfeigned lie fearing God have judged of such men?

I am assured that not only should they have been judged foolish but also enraged, and slaves to Satan, manifestly fighting against God and his appointed order.

The more that I consider the subversion of God's order, which he has placed generally in all living things, the more I do wonder at the blindness of man, who does not consider himself in this case so degenerate that the brute beasts are to be preferred unto him in this behalf.

For nature has in all beasts printed a certain mark of dominion in the male, and a certain subjection in the female, which they keep inviolate. For no man ever saw the lion make obedience, and stoop before the lioness; neither yet can it be proven that the hind takes the conducting of the herd amongst the harts. And yet (alas) man – who by the mouth of God has dominion appointed to him over woman – does not only to his own shame, stoop under the obedience of women, but also in spite of God and of his appointed order, rejoices and maintains that monstrous authority as a thing lawful and just. The insolent joy, the bonefiers, and banqueting, which were in London and elsewhere in England, when that cursed Jezebel was proclaimed queen, did witness to my heart that men were become more than enraged. For else, how could they so have rejoiced at their own confusion and certain destruction? For what man was there of so base judgment (supposing that he had any light of God) who did not see the erecting of that monster to be the overthrow of true religion, and the assured destruction of England, and of the ancient liberties thereof?

And yet nevertheless, all men so triumphed as if God had delivered them from all calamity. But just and righteous, terrible and fearful are thy judgments, O Lord! For as sometimes you did so punish men for unthankfulness,[42] that man [was not] ashamed to commit villainy with man, and that because knowing you to be God, they glorified you not as God; even so, have you most justly now punished the proud rebellion and horrible ingratitude of the realms of England and Scotland.

For when you did offer yourself most mercifully to them both, offering the means by which they might have been joined together forever in godly concord, then was the one proud and cruel, and the other unconstant and fickle of promise. But yet (alas) did miserable England further rebel against you. For albeit you did not cease to heap benefit upon benefit during the reign of an innocent and tender king, yet no man did acknowledge your potent hand and marvelous working. The stout courage of captains, the wit and policy of counselors, the learning of bishops, did rob you of your glory and honor.

For what then was heard as concerning religion, but "The king's proceedings, the king's proceedings must be obeyed"? It is enacted by parliament, therefore it is treason to speak to the contrary. But this was not the end of this miserable tragedy. For you did yet proceed to offer your

---

[42] Romans 1

favors, sending your prophets and messengers to call for reformation of life in all estates.

For even from the highest to the lowest, all were declined from you (yea, even those that should have been the lanterns to others). Some I am assured did quake and tremble, and from the bottom of their hearts thirsted amendment, and for the same purpose did earnestly call for discipline. But then burst forth the venom which before lurked. Then might they not contain their despiteful voices, but with open mouths did cry: "We will not have such a one to reign over us." Then, I say, was every man so stout, that he would not be brought in bondage – no not to you, O Lord, but with disdain did the multitude cast from them the amiable yoke of Christ Jesus. No man would suffer his sin to be rebuked, no man would have his life called to trial.

And thus did they refuse you, O Lord, and your Son Christ Jesus to be their pastor, protector and prince. And therefore have you given them over unto a reprobate mind. You have taken from them the spirit of boldness, of wisdom and of righteous judgment. They see their own destruction, and yet they have no grace to avoid it. Yea, they are become so blind, that knowing the pit, they headlong cast themselves into the same, as the nobility of England, do this day, fighting in the defense of their mortal enemy the Spaniard.

Finally, they are so destitute of understanding and judgment that, although they know that there is a liberty and freedom which their predecessors have enjoyed, yet are they compelled to bow their necks under the yoke of Satan and of his proud ministers, pestilent papists, and proud Spaniards. And yet can they not consider that where a woman reigns and papists bear authority, there must needs Satan be president of the counsel.

Thus have you, O Lord, in your hot displeasure revenged the contempt of your graces offered. But, O Lord, if you shall retain wrath to the end, what flesh is able to sustain? We have sinned, O Lord, and are not worthy to be relieved. But worthy are you, O Lord, to be a true God, and worthy is your Son Christ Jesus, to have his gospel and glory advanced, which both are trodden underfoot in this cruel murder and persecution, which the builders of Babylon commit in their fury, [and] have raised against your children, for the establishing of their kingdom. Let the sobs therefore of your prisoners, O Lord, pass up to your ears, consider their affliction, and let the eyes of your mercy look down upon the blood of such as die for testimony of your eternal verity, and let not your enemies mock your judgment forever.

To you, O Lord, I turn my wretched and wicked heart; to you alone I direct my complaint and groans, for in that [isle] to your saints there is left no comfort. Albeit I have thus (talking with my God in the anguish of my heart) somewhat digressed, yet have I not utterly forgotten my former proposition, to wit, that it is a thing repugnant to the order of nature that any woman be exalted to rule over men. For God has denied unto her the office of a head. And in the entreating of this part, I remember that I have made the nobility both of England and Scotland inferior to brute beasts, for that they do to women, which no male amongst the common sort of beasts can be proven to do to their females, that is: they reverence them, and quake at their presence, they obey their commandments – and that against God. Wherefore I judge them not only subjects to women, but slaves of Satan, and servants of iniquity.

If any man think these my words sharp or vehement, let him consider that the offense is more heinous than can be expressed by words. For where all things are expressly concluded against the glory and honor of God, and where the blood of the saints of God is commanded to be shed, whom shall we judge: God or the devil, to be president of that council? Plain it is that God rules not by his love, mercy, nor grace in the assembly of the ungodly. Then it rests that the devil, the prince of this world, does reign over such tyrants. Whose servants, I pray you, shall then be judged such as obey and execute their tyranny? [May] God for his great mercy's sake, illuminate the eyes of men, that they may perceive into what miserable bondage they are brought, by the monstriferous empire of women.

The second glass which God has set before the eyes of man, wherein he may behold the order which pleases his wisdom concerning authority and dominion, is that commonwealth to which it pleases his majesty to appoint, and give laws, statutes, rites, and ceremonies – not only concerning religion, but also touching their policy and regiment of the same. And against that order it does manifestly repugn that any woman shall occupy the throne of God – that is: the royal seat – which he by his Word has appointed to man, as in giving the law to Israel concerning the election of a king, is evident. For thus it is written: "If thou shalt say, I will appoint a king above me, as the rest of the nations, which are about me, thou shalt make thee a king, whom the Lord thy God shall choose, one from amongst the midst of thy brethren, thou shalt appoint king above thee. Thou mayest not make a stranger that is not thy brother."[43]

Here expressly is a man appointed to be chosen king, and a man native amongst themselves, by which precept are all women and all strangers secluded. What may be objected for the part or election of a stranger, shall be, God-willing, answered in the blast of the second trumpet. For this present, I say that the erecting of a woman to that

---

[43] Deuteronomy 17

honor is not only to invert the order which God has established, but also it is to defile, pollute, and profane (so far as in man lies) the throne and seat of God, which he has sanctified and appointed for man only, in the course of this wretched life, to occupy and possess as his minister and lieutenant, secluding from the same all woman, as before is expressed.

If any think that the fore-written law did bind the Jews only, let the same man consider that the election of a king and appointing of judges, did neither appertain to the ceremonial law, nor yet was it mere judicial, but that it did flow from the moral law as an ordinance, having respect to the conservation of both the tables.

For the office of the magistrate ought to have the first and chief respect to the glory of God, commanded and contained in the former table, as is evident by that which was enjoined to Joshua by God, what time he was accepted and admitted ruler and governor over his people, in these words:[44] "Thou shalt divide the inheritance to this people, the which I have sworn to their fathers, to give unto them; so that thou be valiant and strong, that thou mayest keep and do, according to that whole law, which my servant Moses has commanded thee. Thou shalt not decline from it, neither to the right hand, neither to the left hand, that thou mayest do prudently in all things, that thou takest in hand,

---

[44] Joshua 1

let not the boke of this law depart from thy mouth, but meditate in it, day and night: that thou mayest keep and do, according to everything, that is written in it. For then shall thy ways prosper, and then shalt thou do prudently," etc.[45]

And the same precept gives God by the mouth of Moses, to kings, after they be elected, in these words: "When he shall sit in the throne or seat of his kingdom, he shall write to himself a copy of this law in a book, and that shall be with him, that he may read in it all the days of his life, that he may learn to fear the Lord his God, and to keep all the words of this law, and all these statutes, that he may do them," etc.[46]

Of these two places, it is evident that principally it appertains to the king or to the chief magistrate to know the will of God, to be instructed in his law and statutes, and to promote his glory with his whole heart and study, which are the chief points of the first table.

No man denies but that the sword is committed to the magistrate, to the end that he should punish vice, and maintain virtue: to punish vice, I say, not only that which troubles the tranquility and quiet estate of the commonwealth by adultery, theft, or murder committed, but also such vices as openly impugn the glory of God, as idolatry, blasphemy, and manifest heresy taught and

---

[45] Rulers should take heed to this.
[46] Deuteronomy 17

obstinately maintained, as the histories and notable acts of Hezekiah, Jehoshaphat, and Josiah do plainly teach us, whose study and care was not only to glorify God in their own life and conversation, but also they unfeignedly did travel to bring their subjects to the true worshiping and honoring of God, and did destroy all monuments of idolatry, did punish to death the teachers of it, and removed from office and honors such as were maintainers of those abominations. Whereby, I suppose that it is evident that the office of the king or supreme magistrate has respect to the moral law, and to the conservation of both the tables.

Now if the moral law is the constant and unchangeable will of God, to which the Gentile is no less bound than was the Jew; and if God wills that amongst the Gentiles, the ministers and executors of his law [should] now be appointed, as sometimes they were appointed amongst the Jews; further, if the execution of justice be no less requisite in the policy of the Gentiles than ever it was amongst the Jews, then what man can be so foolish to suppose or believe that God will now admit those persons to sit in judgment or to reign over men in the commonwealth of the Gentiles, whom he by his expressed Word and ordinance did before debar and seclude from the same?

And that women were secluded from the royal seat, which ought to be the sanctuary to all poor afflicted, and therefore is justly called *the seat of God* (besides the place before recited of the election of a king, and besides the places of the New Testament, which is most evident), the order and election which was kept in Judah and Israel, does manifestly declare. For when the males of the kingly stock failed, as often as it chanced in Israel and sometimes in Judah, it never entered into the hearts of the people of chose and promote to honors any of the king's daughters (had he never so many); but knowing God's vengeance to be poured forth upon the father by the taking away of his sons, they had no further respect to his stock, but elected such one man or other as they judged most apt for that honor and authority.

Of these premises, I conclude (as before) that to promote a woman head over men is repugnant to nature, and a thing most contrarious to that order which God has approved in that commonwealth, which he did institute and rule by his Word. But now to the last point, to wit: that *the empire of a woman is a thing repugnant to justice and the destruction of every commonwealth where it is received*; in probation whereof, because the matter is more than evident, I will use few words:

- First, I say, if justice is a constant and perpetual will to give to every person, their own right (as the most learned in all ages have defined it to be) then to give or to will to give to any

- person that which is not their right, must repugn to justice.
- But to reign above man can never be the right to woman, because it is a thing denied unto her by God, as is before declared.
- Therefore, to promote her to that estate or dignity, can be nothing else but repugnancy to justice.

If I should speak no more, this would be sufficient. For except that either they can improve the definition of justice, or else that they can entreat God to revoke and call back his sentence pronounced against woman, they shall be compelled to admit my conclusion. If any find fault with justice, as it is defined, he may well accuse others, but me he shall not hurt. For I have the shield, the weapon, and the warrant of him, who assuredly will defend this quarrel, and he commands me to cry:

- Whatsoever repugns to the will of God expressed in his most sacred Word, repugns to justice.
- But that women have authority over men repugns to the will of God expressed in his Word.
- And therefore my author commands me to conclude without fear, that all such authority repugns to justice.

The first part of the argument I trust dare neither Jew nor Gentile deny, for it is a principle not only universally confessed, but also so deeply printed in the heart of man, be his nature never so corrupted, that whether he will or not, he his compelled at one time or other, to acknowledge and confess that justice is violated when things are done against the will of God expressed by his Word.

And to this confession are no less the reprobate coacted and constrained than are the chosen children of God, albeit to a [different] end. The elect – with displeasure of their fact [*deed*] – confess their offense, having access to grace and mercy, as did Adam, David, Peter, and all other penitent offenders. But the reprobate – notwithstanding they are compelled to acknowledge the will of God to be just [that] which they have offended – yet are they never inwardly displeased with their iniquity, but rage, complain and storm against God, whose vengeance they cannot escape, as did Cain, Judas, Herod, Julian called *apostata*; yea, Jezebel, and Athaliah.[47] For Cain no doubt was convicted in conscience that he had done against justice in murdering his brother. Judas did openly before the high priest confess that he had sinned in betraying innocent blood. Herod – being stricken by the angel – did mock those his flatterers, saying unto them: "Behold your god (meaning himself) cannot now preserve himself from corruption and worms."

---

[47] Genesis 4, Matthew 27

Julianus was compelled in the end to cry, "O Galilean," (so always in contempt did he name our Savior Jesus Christ), "You have now overcome!" And who doubts but Jezebel and Athaliah, before their miserable end, were convicted in their cankered consciences to acknowledge that the murder which they had committed, and the empire which the one had [for] six years usurped, were repugnant to justice?

Even so shall they – I doubt not – who this day do possess and maintain that monstriferous authority of women, shortly be compelled to acknowledge that their studies and devices have been bent against God, and that all such authority as women have usurped, repugns to justice, because, as I have said, it repugns to the will of God expressed in his sacred Word.

And if any man [should] doubt hereof, let him mark well the words of the apostle, saying: "I permit not a woman to teach, neither yet to usurp authority above man."[48] No man I trust will deny these words of the apostle to be the will of God expressed in his Word, and he says openly: "I permit not," etc., which is as much as, "I will not that a woman have authority, charge or power over man." For so much imports the Greek word αὐθεντεῖν in that place. Now let man and angel conspire against God, let them pronounce their laws, and say "We will suffer women to bear authority;" who then can depose them? Yet shall

---

[48] 1 Timothy 2

this one word of the eternal God spoken by the mouth of a weak man, thrust them each one into hell.

Jezebel may for a time sleep quietly in the bed of her fornication and whoredom, she may teach and deceive for a season; but neither shall she preserve herself, nor yet her adulterous children from great affliction, and from the sword of God's vengeance, which shall shortly apprehend such works of iniquity.[49] The admonition I defer to the end.

Here might I bring in the oppression and injustice, which is committed against realms and nations, which sometimes lived free, and now are brought in bondage of foreign nations by the reason of this monstriferous authority and empire of women. But that I delay until a better opportunity. And now I think it expedient to answer such objections as carnal and worldly men – yea men ignorant of God – use [*tend*] to make for maintenance of this tyranny (authority it is not worthy to be called) and most unjust empire of woman.

First they do object the examples of Deborah, and of Huldah the prophetess, of whom the one judged Israel, and the other, by all appearance, did teach and exhort. Secondarily, they do object the law made by Moses for the daughters of Zelophehad.[50] Thirdly, the consent of the

---

[49] Revelation 2
[50] Numbers 27

estates of such realms as have approved the empire and regiment of women. And last, the long custom which has received the regiment of women, their valiant acts and prosperity, together with some papistical laws which have confirmed the same.

To the first, I answer that particular examples do establish no common law. The causes were known to God alone, why he took the spirit of wisdom and force from all men of those ages, and did so mightily assist women against nature, and against his ordinary course, that the one he made a deliverer to his afflicted people Israel, and to the other he gave not only perseverance in the true religion, when the most part of men had declined from the same. But also to her he gave the spirit of prophecy to assure King Josiah of the things which were to come. With these women, I say, did God work potently and miraculously – yea, to them he gave most singular grace and privilege.

But who has commanded that a public – yea, a tyrannical and most wicked law be established upon these examples? The men who object the same are not altogether ignorant that examples have no strength when the question is of law. As if I should ask, *what marriage is lawful?*, and it should be answered that it is lawful to man not only to have many wives at once, but also it is lawful to marry two sisters, and to enjoy them both living at once, because David, Jacob, and Solomon, servants of God did the same, I trust that no man would justify the vanity of this reason. Or if the question were demanded, [whether] a Christian with good conscience may defraud, steal or deceive, and answer were made that so he might by the example of the Israelites who at God's commandment deceived the Egyptians and spoiled them of their garments, gold and silver, I think likewise this reason should be mocked.

And what greater force, I pray you, has the former argument?

- Deborah did rule in Israel, and Huldah spoke prophecy in Judah.
- Ergo, it is lawful for women to reign above realms and nations, or to teach in the presence of men.

The consequent is vain and of none effect. For of examples, as is before declared, we may establish no law, but we are always bound to the law written, and to the commandment expressed in the same. And the law – written and pronounced by God – forbids no less that any woman reign over man than it forbids man to take plurality of wives, to marry two sisters living at once, to steal, to rob, to murder or to lie. If any of these has been transgressed, and yet God has not imputed the same, it makes not the like fact or deed lawful unto us. For God – being free – may for such causes as be approved by his inscrutable wisdom, dispense with the rigor of his law, and may use his creatures at his pleasure. But the same power is not permitted to man, whom he has made subject to his law, and not to the examples of fathers. And this I think sufficient to the reasonable and moderate spirits.

But to repress the raging of woman's madness, I will descend somewhat deeper in to the matter, and not fear to affirm that as we find a contrary spirit in all these most wicked women that this day are exalted into this tyrannous authority to the spirit that was in those godly matrons, so I fear not, I say, to affirm that their condition is unlike, and that their end shall be diverse.

In those matrons, we find that the spirit of mercy, truth, justice, and humility did reign. Under them, we find that God did show mercy to his people, delivering them from the tyranny of strangers, and from the venom of idolatry by the hands and counsel of those women.

But in these of our ages, we find cruelty, [falsehood], pride, covetousness, deceit, and oppression. In them we also find the spirit of Jezebel and Athaliah. Under them, we find the simple people oppressed, the true religion extinguished, and the blood of Christ's members most cruelly shed. And finally, by their practices and deceit, we find ancient realms and nations given and betrayed into the hands of strangers, the titles and liberties of them taken from the just possessors. This one thing is an evident testimony of how unlike our mischievous Marys are unto Deborah, under whom were strangers chased out of Israel: God so raising her up to be a mother and deliverer to his oppressed people.

But (alas), he has raised up these Jezebels to be the uttermost of his plagues, which man's unthankfulness has long deserved. But his secret and most just judgment shall neither excuse them nor their maintainers, because their counsels are diverse. But to prosecute my purpose, let such as list [*wish*] to defend these monsters in their tyranny, prove first that their sovereign mistresses are like Deborah in godliness and pity; and secondarily, that the same success does follow their tyranny, which did follow the extraordinary regiment of that godly matron. This thing, [even if] they were able to do [it] (as they never shall be, let them blow till they burst), yet shall her example profit them nothing at all. For they are never able to prove that either Deborah or any other godly woman (having the commendation of the Holy Ghost within the Scriptures) has usurped authority above any realm or nation by reason of their birth and blood.

Neither yet did they claim it by right or inheritance, but God – by his singular privilege, favor, and grace – exempted Deborah from the common malediction given to women in that behalf, and against nature he made her prudent in counsel, strong in courage, happy in regiment, and a blessed mother and deliverer to his people. This he did partly to advance and notify the power of his majesty as well to his enemies, as to his own people, in that he declared himself able to give salvation and deliverance by means of the most weak vessels; and partly he did it to confound and shame all men of that age, because they had for the most part declined from his true obedience. And therefore was the spirit of courage, regiment, and boldness taken from them for a time to their confusion and further humiliation. But what makes this for Mary and her match Philip?

One thing I would ask of such as depend upon the example of Deborah: whether she was widow or wife when she judged Israel, and when that God gave that notable victory to his people under her? If they answer she was a widow, I would lay against them the testimony of the Holy Ghost, witnessing that she was wife to Lapidoth.[51] And if they will shift, and allege that so she might be called, notwithstanding that her husband was dead, I urge them further that they are not able to prove it to be any common phrase and manner of speech in the Scriptures that a woman shall be called the wife of a dead man, except that there [should] be some note added, whereby it may be known that her husband is departed, as is witnessed of Anna. But in this place of the Judges, there is no note added, that her husband [is] dead, but rather the expressed contrary.

---

[51] Judges 4

For the text says: "In that time, a woman named Deborah a prophetess, wife to Lapidoth, judged Israel." The Holy Ghost plainly speaks that [at the] time she judged Israel, she was wife to Lapidoth. If she were wife, and if she ruled all alone in Israel, then I ask: Why did she not prefer her husband to that honor to be captain, and to be leader to the host of the Lord? If any think that it was her husband, the text proves the contrary, for it affirms that Barak of the tribe of Naphtali was appointed to that office. If Barak had been her husband, to what purpose should the Holy Ghost so diligently have noted the tribe, and another name than was before expressed? Yea, to what purpose should it be noted, that she send and called him? Whereof I doubt not but that every reasonable man does consider that this Barak was not her husband.

And thereof likewise, it is evident that her judgment or government in Israel was no such usurped power as our queens unjustly possess this day; but that it was the spirit of prophecy which rested upon her, [at which] time the multitude of the people had wrought wickedly in the eyes of the Lord, by which spirit she did rebuke the idolatry and iniquity of the people, exhort them to repentance, and in the end, did bring them this comfort: that God [would] deliver them from the bondage and thralldom of their enemies. And this she might do, notwithstanding that another did occupy the place of the supreme magistrate (if any was in those days in Israel), for so I find did Huldah the wife of Shallum in the days of Josiah king of Judah speak prophecy and comfort the king; and yet he resigned to her neither the scepter nor the sword.[52]

That this our interpretation how Deborah did judge in Israel is the true meaning of the Holy Ghost, the pondering and weighing of the history shall manifestly prove. When she sends for Barak, I pray you, in whose name does she give him his charge? Does she speak to him as kings and princes use [*tend*] to speak to their subjects in such cases? No, but she speaks as she who had a special revelation from God, which neither was known to Barak nor to the people, saying: "Has not the Lord God of Israel commanded thee?" This is her preface, by which she would stir up the dull senses of Barak and of the people, willing to persuade unto them that the time was come when God would show himself their protector and deliverer, in which preface she usurps to herself neither power nor authority.

For she says not: "I being thy princess, thy mistress, thy sovereign lady and queen, command thee upon thine allegiance, and under pain of treason to go, and gather an army." No, she spoils herself of all power to command, attributing that authority to God, of whom she had her revelation and certitude to appoint Barak captain, which afterwards appears more plainly. For when she had declared

---

[52] 2 Kings 22

to him the whole counsel of God, appointing unto him as well the number of his soldiers, as the tribes out of which they should be gathered. And when she had appointed the place of the battle (which she could not have done, but by especial revelation of God) and had assured him of victory in the name of God, and yet that he fainted and openly refused to enter into that journey except that the prophetess would accompany him, she did use against him no external power, she did not threaten him with rebellion and death, but for assurance of his faint heart and weak conscience, being content to go with him, she pronounces that the glory should not be his in that journey, but that the Lord should fell Sisera into the hand of a woman.

Such as have more pleasure in light than in darkness may clearly perceive that Deborah did usurp no such power nor authority, as our queens do this day claim; but [rather], she was endued with the spirit of wisdom, of knowledge, and of the true fear of God, and by the same she judged the facts of the rest of the people. She rebuked their defection and idolatry – yea, and also did redress to her power the injuries that were done by man to man. But all this, I say, she did by the spiritual sword, that is: by the Word of God, and not by any temporal regiment or authority, which she did usurp over Israel.

In this, I suppose, at that time there was no lawful magistrate, by the reason of their great affliction. For so witnesses the history, saying: "And Ehud being dead, the Lord sold Israel into the hand of Jabin king of Canaan. And he by Sisera his captain afflicted Israel greatly the space of twenty years." And Deborah herself, in her song of thanksgiving, confesses that before she did arise mother in Israel, and in the days of Jael, there was nothing but confusion and trouble.

If any sticks to the term, alleging that the Holy Ghost says that she judged Israel, let them understand that neither does the Hebrew word nor yet the Latin always signify *civil judgment*, or *the execution of the temporal sword*, but most commonly is taken in the sense which we have before expressed. For of Christ it is said: "He shall judge many nations." And that: "He shall pronounce judgment to the Gentiles."[53] And yet it is evident that he was no minister of the temporal sword. God commands Jerusalem and Judah to judge between him and his vineyard, and yet he appointed not them all to be civil magistrates. To Ezekiel, it is said: "Shalt thou not judge them son of man?" and after: "Thou son of man, shalt thou not judge? Shalt thou not judge, I say, the city of blood?" And also: "Behold, I shall judge betwixt beast and beast."[54] And such places in great number are to be found throughout the whole Scriptures. And yet I trust no man will be so foolish as to think that

---

[53] Isaiah 2, Isaiah 42, Micah 5, Isaiah 5.
[54] Ezekiel 20, 22, 34

any of the prophets were appointed by God to be political judges, or to punish the sins of man by corporal punishment.

No, the manner of their judgment is expressed in these words: "Declare to them all their abominations, and thou shalt say to them: Thus says the Lord God: a city shedding blood in the midst of her, that her time may approach and which has made idols against herself, that she might be polluted. Thou hast transgressed in the blood which thou hast shed, and thou art polluted in the idols, which thou hast made."[55] Thus, I say, do the prophets of God judge, pronouncing the sentence of God against malefactors.

And so I doubt not but Deborah judged what time Israel had declined from God, rebuking their defection and exhorting them to repentance, without usurpation of any civil authority. And if the people gave unto her for a time any reverence or honor as her godliness and happy counsel did well deserve, yet was it no such empire as our monsters claim. For which of her sons or nearest kinsmen did she leave as ruler and judge in Israel after her? The Holy Ghost expresses no such thing. Whereof it is evident that by her example, God offers no occasion to establish any regiment of women above men, realms, and nations.

But now to the second objection. In this, women require (as to them appears) nothing but equity and justice,

---

[55] Ezekiel 22

whilst they and their patrons for them require dominion and empire above men. For this is their question: *Is it not lawful that women have their right and inheritance, like as the daughters of Zalphead were commanded by the mouth of Moses to have their portion of ground in their tribe?*

I answer, it is not only lawful that women possess their inheritance, but I affirm also that justice and equity require that so they do. But therewith I add that which gladly they list not understand: that *to bear rule or authority over man, can never be right nor inheritance to woman.*

- For that can never be just inheritance to any person, which God by his Word has plainly denied unto them.
- But to all women has God denied authority above man, as most manifestly is before declared.
- Therefore to her it can never be inheritance.

And thus must the advocates of our ladies provide some better example and stronger argument. For the law made in favor of the daughters of Zelophehad will serve them nothing. And assuredly, great wonder it is that in so great light of God's truth, men list to grope and wander in darkness. For let them speak of conscience; if the petition of any of these aforenamed women was to reign over any one tribe – yea, or yet over any one man within Israel – plain it is, they did not, but only required that they might have a portion of ground among the men of their tribe, lest that the name of their father should be abolished. And this was granted unto them without respect had to any civil regiment.

And what makes this, I pray you, for the establishing of this monstrous empire of women? The question is not if women may not succeed to possession, substance, patrimony or inheritance, such as fathers may leave to their children, for that I willingly grant; but the question is if women may succeed to their fathers in offices, and chiefly to that office, the executor whereof does occupy the place and throne of God. And that I absolutely deny, and fear not to say that to place a woman in authority above a realm is to pollute and profane the royal seat, the throne of justice, which ought to be the throne of God; and that to maintain them in the same is nothing else but continually to rebel against God.

One thing there is yet to be noted and observed in the law made concerning the inheritance of the daughters of Zelophehad, to wit: that it was forbidden unto them to marry without their own tribe, lest that such portion as fell to their lot should be transferred from one tribe to another, and so should the tribe of Manasseh be defrauded and spoiled of their just inheritance by their occasion.[56] For the avoiding of this, it was commanded by Moses that they

---

[56] Numbers 36

should marry in the family or household of the tribe and kindred of their father. Wonder it is that the advocates and patrons of the right of our ladies did not consider and ponder this law before they counseled the blind princes and unworthy nobles of their countries to betray the liberties thereof into the hands of strangers.

England – for satisfying the inordinate appetites of that cruel monster Mary (unworthy by reason of her bloody tyranny, of the name of a *woman*) – betrayed (alas) to the proud Spaniard; and Scotland by the rash madness of foolish governors, and by the practices of a crafty dame resigned likewise, under title of marriage in to the power of France. Does such translation of realms and nations please the justice of God, or is the possession by such means obtained, lawful in his sight? Assured I am that it is not.

No otherwise, I say, then is that possession, whereunto thieves, murderers, tyrants, and oppressors do attain by theft, murder, tyranny, violence, deceit, and oppression, which God of his secret (but yet most just) judgment does often permit for punishment, as well of the sufferers, as of the violent oppressors, but does never approve the same as lawful and godly.

For if he would not permit that the inheritance of the children of Israel should pass from one tribe to another by the marriage of any daughter, notwithstanding that they were all one people, all spoke one tongue, all were descended of one father, and all did profess one God, and one religion; if yet, I say, God would not suffer that the commodity and usual fruit which might be gathered of the portion of ground limited and assigned to one tribe should pass to another; will he suffer that the liberties, laws, commodities and fruits of whole realms and nations are given into the power and distribution of others by the reason of marriage, and in the powers of such, as besides that they are of a strange tongue, of strange manners and laws, they are also ignorant of God, enemies to his truth, deniers of Christ Jesus, persecutors of his true members, and haters of all virtue? As the odious nation of Spaniards does manifestly declare, who for the very spite which they do bear against Christ Jesus, whom their forefathers did crucify (for Jews they are, as histories do witness, and they themselves confess), do this day make plain war against all true professors of his holy gospel.[57]

And how blindly and outrageously the French king and his pestilent prelates do fight against the verity of God, the flaming fires which lick up the innocent blood of Christ's members do witness, and by his cruel edicts is notified and proclaimed.[58]

---

[57] The Spaniards are Jews and they brag that Mary of England is the root of Jesse.
[58] Note the law which he has proclaimed in France against such as he terms *Lutherans*.

And yet to these two cruel tyrants (to France and Spain, I mean) is the right and possession of England and Scotland appointed. But just or lawful shall that possession never be, until God does change the statute of his former law, which he will not do for the pleasure of man. For he has not created the earth to satisfy the ambition of two or three tyrants,[59] but for the universal seed of Adam, and has appointed and defined the bounds of their habitation to diverse nations, assigning diverse countries as he himself confesses, speaking to Israel in these words: "You shall pass by the bounds and limits of your brethren the sons of Esau, who dwell in Mount Seir. They shall fear you. But take diligent heed, that ye show not yourselves cruel against them. For I will give you no part of their land. No not the breadth of a foot. For Mount Seir I have given to Esau to be possessed."[60]

And the same he does witness of the sons of Lot, to whom he had given Ar to be possessed. And Moses plainly affirms that when the Almighty did distribute and divide possessions to the Gentiles, and when he did disperse and scatter the sons of men, that then he did appoint the limits and bounds of peoples for the number of the sons of Israel.[61] Whereof it is plain that God has not exposed the earth in prey to tyrants, making all thing lawful, which by violence

---

[59] Acts 17
[60] Deuteronomy 2
[61] Deuteronomy 32

and murder they may possess, but that he has appointed to every several nation a several possession, willing them to stand content (as nature did teach an ethnic to affirm)[62] with that portion which by lot and just means they had enjoyed.

For what causes God permits this his distribution to be troubled, and the realms of ancient nations to be possessed of strangers, I delay at this time to entreat. Only this I have recited to give the world to understand: that the reign, empire, and authority of women, has no ground within God's Scriptures. Yea, that realms or provinces possessed by their marriage, is nothing but unjust conquest. For so little does the law made for the daughters of Zelophehad help the cause of your queens, that utterly it fights against them, both damning their authority and fact.

But now to the third objection. The consent, say they, of realms and laws pronounced and admitted in this behalf, long consuetude and custom, together with the felicity of some women in their empires have established their authority. To whom I answer that neither may the tyranny of princes, nor the foolishness of people, nor wicked laws made against God, nor yet the felicity that in this earth may hereof insue, make that thing lawful which he by his Word has manifestly condemned.

---

[62] Cicero *De Officiis*, Book 1

For if the approbation of princes and people, laws made by men, or the consent of realms, may establish anything against God and his Word, then should idolatry be preferred to the true religion. For more realms and nations, more laws and decrees published by emperors with common consent of their counsels, have established the one, than have approved the other. And yet I think that no man of sound judgment will therefore justify and defend idolatry. No more ought any man to maintain this odious empire of women, although that it were approved of all men by their laws. For the same God that in plain words forbids idolatry, does also forbid the authority of women over man, as the words of Saint Paul before rehearsed do plainly teach us. And therefore whether women are deposed from that unjust authority (have they never usurped it so long) or if all such honor is denied unto them, I fear not to affirm that they are neither defrauded of right nor inheritance. For to women can that honor never be due nor lawful (much less inheritance) which God has so manifestly denied unto them.

I am not ignorant that the subtle wits of carnal men (which can never be brought under the obedience of God's simple precepts to maintain this monstrous empire) have yet two vain shifts.

First they allege that albeit women may not absolutely reign by themselves, because they may neither fit in judgment, nor pronounce sentence, nor execute any public office; yet may they do all such things by their lieutenants, deputies, and substitute judges.

Secondarily, say they, a woman born to rule over any realm may choose her a husband, and to him she may transfer and give her authority and right. To both I answer in few words: First, that from a corrupt and venomed fountain can spring no wholesome water. Secondarily, that:

- No person has power to give the thing which does not justly appertain to themselves.
- But the authority of a woman is a corrupted fountain, and therefore from her can never spring any lawful officer. She is not born to rule over men, and therefore she can appoint none by her gift, nor by her power (which she has not) to the place of a lawful magistrate.
- And therefore whosoever receives of a woman, office or authority, are adulterous and bastard officers before God.[63]

This may appear strange at the first affirmation, but if we will be as indifferent and equal in the cause of God as that we can be in the cause of man, the reason shall suddenly appear.

The case supposed that a tyrant by conspiracy usurped the royal seat and dignity of a king, and in the same did so

---

[63] Let England and Scotland take heed

establish himself, that he appointed officers, and did what him list for a time; and in this meantime, the native king made straight inhibition to all his subjects that none should adhere to this traitor, neither yet receive any dignity of him, yet nevertheless they would honor the same traitor as king, and become his officers in all affairs of the realm.

If after, the native prince did recover his just honor and possession, should he repute or esteem any man of the traitors appointment for a lawful magistrate? Or for his friend and true subject? Or should he not rather with one sentence condemn the head with the members? And if so he should do, who [would be] able to accuse him of rigor? Much less to condemn his sentence of injustice. And dare we deny the same power to God in the like case?

For that woman reigns above man, she has obtained it by treason and conspiracy committed against God. How can it be then that she – being criminal and guilty of treason against God committed – can appoint any officer pleasing in his sight? It is a thing impossible. Wherefore let men that receive of women authority, honor, or office, be most assuredly persuaded that in so maintaining that usurped power, they declare themselves enemies to God.

If any think that because the realm and estates thereof have given their consents to a woman, and have established her and her authority, that therefore it is lawful and acceptable before God, let the same men remember what I have said before, to wit: that God cannot approve the doing nor consent of any multitude, concluding anything against his Word and ordinance. And therefore they must have a more assured defense against the wrath of God than the approbation and consent of a blinded multitude, or else they shall not be able to stand in the presence of the consuming fire. That is, they must acknowledge that the regiment of a woman is a thing most odious in the presence of God. They must refuse to be her officers, because she is a traitoress and rebel against God. And finally, they must study to repress her inordinate pride and tyranny to the uttermost of their power.

The same is the duty of the nobility and estates, by whose blindness a woman is promoted. First, insofar as they have most heinously offended against God, placing in authority such as God by his Word has removed from the same, unfeignedly they ought to call for mercy, and being admonished of their error and damnable fact, in sign and token of true repentance, with common consent they ought to retreat that which unadvisedly and by ignorance they have pronounced, and ought without further delay to remove from authority all such persons, as by usurpation, violence, or tyranny, do possess the same.

For so did Israel and Judah after they had revolted from David, and Judah alone in the days of Athaliah.[64] For after

---

[64] 2 Kings 11

she by murdering her son's children had obtained the empire over the land, and had most unhappily reigned in Judah six years, Jehoiada the high priest called together the captains and chief rulers of the people, and showing to them the king's son Joash, did bind them by an oath to depose that wicked woman, and to promote the king to his royal seat, which they faithfully did, killing at his commandment not only that cruel and mischievous woman, but also the people did destroy the temple of Baal, break his altars and images, and kill Mattan, Baal's high priest, before his altars.[65]

The same is the duty as well of the estates as of the people that have been blinded. First, they ought to remove from honor and authority that monster in nature (so call I a woman clad in the habit of man – yea, a woman against nature reigning above man). Secondarily, if any presume to defend that impiety, they ought not to fear, first to pronounce, and then after to execute against them the sentence of death. If any man is afraid to violate the oath of obedience which they have made to such monsters, let them be most assuredly persuaded that as the beginning of their oaths proceeding from ignorance was sin, so is the obstinate purpose to keep the same, nothing but plain rebellion against God. But of this matter, in *the second blast*, God-willing, we shall speak more at large.

---

[65] Mark this fact, for it agrees with God's pronounced law.

And now to put an end to *the first blast*, seeing that by the order of nature, by the malediction and curse pronounced against woman, by the mouth of St. Paul the interpreter of God's sentence, by the example of that commonwealth, in which God by his Word planted order and policy, and finally by the judgment of the most godly writers, God has dejected woman from rule, dominion, empire, and authority above man.

Moreover, seeing that neither the example of Deborah, nor the law made for the daughters of Zelophehad, nor yet the foolish consent of an ignorant multitude, is able to justify that which God so plainly has condemned, let all men take heed what quarrel and cause from hence further they do defend. If God raises up any noble heart to vindicate the liberty of his country, and to suppress the monstrous empire of women, let all such as shall presume to defend them in the same, most certainly know that in so doing, they lift their hand against God, and that one day they shall find his power to fight against their foolishness.

Let not the faithful, godly, and valiant hearts of Christ's soldiers be utterly discouraged, nor yet let the tyrants rejoice, albeit for a time they triumph against such as study to repress their tyranny, and to remove them from unjust authority.

For the causes alone why he suffers the soldiers to fail in battle whom nevertheless he commands to fight as sometimes did Israel fighting against Benjamin – the cause of the Israelites was most just, for it was to punish that horrible abomination of those sons of Belial, abusing the Levite's wife, whom the Benjamites did defend; and they had God's precept to assure them of well doing, for he did not only command them to fight, but also appointed Judah to be their leader and captain, and yet fell they twice in plain battle against those most wicked adulterers[66] – the secret cause of this, I say, is known to God alone.

But by his evident Scriptures, we may assuredly gather that by such means does his wisdom sometimes beat down the pride of the flesh (for the Israelites at the first trusted in their multitude, power and strength), and sometimes by such overthrows, he will punish the offenses of his own children, and bring them to the unfeigned knowledge of the same, before he will give them victory against the manifest contemners, whom he has appointed nevertheless to uttermost perdition, as the end of that battle did witness.

For although with great murder the children of Israel did twice fall before the Benjamites, yet after they had wept before the Lord, after they had fasted and made sacrifice in sign of their unfeigned repentance, they so prevailed against that proud tribe of Benjamin, that after 25,000 strong men of war were killed in battle, they destroyed man, woman, child and beast, as well in the fields as in the

---

[66] Judges 20

cities, which all were burned with fire, so that only of that whole tribe remained 600 men, who fled to the wilderness, where they remained four months, and so were saved.[67] The same God who did execute this grievous punishment – even by the hands of those whom he suffered twice to be overcome in battle – does this day retain his power and justice. Cursed Jezebel of England, with the pestilent and detestable generation of papists, make no little brag and boast that they have triumphed not only against Wyatt, but also against all such as have enterprised anything against them or their proceedings.

But let her and them consider that yet they have not prevailed against God. His throne is more high than that the length of their horns is able to reach. And let them further consider that in the beginning of this their bloody reign, the harvest of their iniquity was not come to full maturity and ripeness. No, it was so green, so secret I mean, so covered, and so hidden with hypocrisy, that some men (even the servants of God) thought it not impossible, but that wolves might be changed into lambs, and also that the viper might remove her natural venom.

But God, who does reveal in his time appointed the secrets of hearts, and that will have his judgments justified even by the very wicked, has now given open testimony of her and their beastly cruelty. For man and woman, learned

---

[67] Judges 20

and unlearned, nobles and men of baser sort, aged fathers and tender damsels, and finally the bones of the dead, as well women as men have tasted of their tyranny, so that now not only the blood of father Latimer, of the mild man of God the bishop of Canterbury, of learned and discrete Ridley, of innocent Lady Jane Dudley, and many godly and worthy preachers that cannot be forgotten, such as fire has consumed, and the sword of tyranny most unjustly has shed, does call for vengeance in the ears of the Lord God of Hosts; but also the sobs and tears of the poor oppressed, the groanings of the angels, the watchmen of the Lord – yea, and every earthly creature abused by their tyranny do continually cry and call for the hasty execution of the same.

I fear not to say that the day of vengeance, which shall apprehend that horrible monster Jezebel of England, and such as maintain her monstrous cruelty, is already appointed in the counsel of the Eternal, and I verily believe that it is so nigh that she shall not reign so long in tyranny as hitherto she has done, when God shall declare himself to be her enemy, when he shall pour forth contempt upon her, according to her cruelty, and shall kindle the hearts of such, as sometimes did favor her with deadly hatred against her, that they may execute his judgments.

And therefore let such as assist her take heed what they do. For assuredly, her empire and reign is a wall without foundation. I mean the same of the authority of all women.

It has been under-propped this blind time that is past, with the foolishness of people, and with the wicked laws of ignorant and tyrannical princes. But the fire of God's Word is already laid to those rotten props (I include the pope's law with the rest), and presently they burn, albeit we espy not the flame. When they are consumed (as shortly they will be, for stubble and dry timber cannot long endure the fire), that rotten wall, the usurped and unjust empire of women, shall fall by itself in spite of all man, to the destruction of so many, as shall labor to uphold it. And therefore let all man be advertised [*notified*], for the trumpet has once blown.

Praise God ye that fear him.

SUMMARY OF THE PROPOSED SECOND BLAST OF THE TRUMPET

JOHN KNOX TO THE READER

ECAUSE many are offended at *The First Blast of the Trumpet*, in which I affirm that to promote a woman to bear rule or empire above any realm, nation, or city, is repugnant to nature, contumely [*an insult*] to God, and a thing most contrary to his revealed and approved ordinance; and because also, that some have promised (as I understand) a confutation of the same, I have delayed *The Second Blast* until such time as their reasons appear, by which I either may be reformed in opinion, else shall have further occasion more simply and plainly to utter my judgment. Yet in the meantime, for the discharge of my conscience, and for avoiding suspicion, which might be engendered by reason of my silence, I could not cease to notify these subsequent propositions, which, by God's grace, I purpose to treat in *The Second Blast* promised.

1. It is not birth only, nor propinquity of blood, that makes a king lawfully to reign above a people professing Christ Jesus and his eternal verity; but in his election must the ordinance which God has established in the election of inferior judges be observed.

2. No manifest idolater, nor notorious transgressor of God's holy precepts, ought to be promoted to any public regiment [government], honor, or dignity, in any realm, province, or city that has subjected itself to his blessed gospel.

3. Neither can oath nor promise bind any such people to obey and maintain tyrants against God and against his truth known.

4. But if either rashly they have promoted any manifestly wicked person, or yet ignorantly have chosen such a one, as after declares himself unworthy of regiment above the people of God (and such be all idolaters and cruel persecutors), most justly may the same men depose and punish him, that unadvisedly before they did nominate, appoint, and elect.

> "If the eye be single, the whole body shall be clear"
> (Matthew 6:22).

APPENDIX.

JOHN KNOX'S APOLOGETICAL DEFENSE OF HIS FIRST BLAST, ETC., TO QUEEN ELIZABETH.

JULY 12th, 1559.
JOHN KNOX to Sir WILLIAM CECIL.

THE spirit of wisdom heal your heart to the glory of God and to the comfort of his afflicted mind.

One cause of my present writing is right honorable humbly to require you to deliver this other lettre enclosed to the queen's grace, [which] contains in few and simple words my confession what I think of her authority, how far it is just, and what may make it odious in God's presence.

I hear there is a confutation set forth in print against *The First Blast*. God grant that the writer have no more sought the favors of the world, no less the glory of God and the stable commodity of his country than did him who interprised in that blast to utter his conscience. When I shall have time (which now is dear and strait unto me) to peruse that work I will communicate my judgment with you concerning the same.

The time is now, Sir, that all that either trust Christ Jesus [reign] in this isle, the liberties of the same to be kept, to the inhabitants thereof, and their hearts to be joined together in love unfeigned ought rather to study how the same may be brought to pass then vainly to travail for the maintenance of that whereof already we have seen the danger, and felt the smart.

State Papers, Scotland, Vol. Art. 57.
In Public Record office, London.

JOHN KNOX'S DECLARATION TO QUEEN ELIZABETH.

JULY 20th, 1559

O the virtuous and godly **Elizabeth** by the grace of **God**, Queen of England, etc., **John Knox** desires the perpetual increase of the Holy Spirit. etc.

As your grace's displeasure against me most unjustly [conceived], has been and is to my wretched heart a burden grievous and almost intolerable, so is the testimony of a clean conscience to me a stay and uphold that in desperation I sink not, however vehement the temptations appear, for in God's presence my conscience bears me record that maliciously nor of purpose I offended your grace, nor your realm. And therefore, however I am judged by man, I am assured to be absolved by him who only knows the secrets of hearts.

I cannot deny the writing of a book against the usurped authority and unjust regiment of women, neither yet am I minded to retract or to call any principal point or proposition of the same, till truth and verity do further appear, but why that either Your Grace, either [that only] such as unfeignedly favors liberty of England should be offended at the author of such a work, I can perceive no just occasion.

For first, my book touches not Your Grace's person [specifically], neither is it prejudicial [to] any liberty of the realm, if the time and my writing are indifferently considered. How could I be enemy to Your Grace's person? For deliverance whereof, I did more study, and enterprise further than any of those that now accuse me.

And as concerning your regiment how could or can I envy that which most I have trusted and for which (as oblivion will suffer) I render thanks unfeignedly unto God, that is, that it has pleased him of his eternal goodness to exalt your head (which times [were] in danger) to the manifestation of his glory and extirpation of idolatry.

And as for any offense which I have committed against England either in writing that or of any other work, I will not refuse that moderate and indifferent men judge and discern between me and those that accuse me. To wit, [which] of the parties do most hurt the liberty of England: I who affirm that no woman may be exalted above any realm to make the liberty of the same thrall to a strange, proud, and evil nation, or those who approve whatsoever pleases princes for the time?

If I were were as well disposed to accuse, as some of them (to their own scheme) have declared themselves I nothing doubt but that in few words I should let reasonable men understand that some that this day lowly crouch to Your Grace, and labor to make me odious in your eyes, did in your adversity neither show themselves faithful friends to Your Grace, nor [were they] so loving and careful over their native country as now they would be esteemed.

But omitting the accusation of others for my own purgation and for Your Grace's satisfaction, I say that nothing in my book conceived is, or can be prejudicial to Your Grace's just regiment, provided that ye be not found ingrate unto God.

Ingrate you shall be proven in presence of his throne, (however that flatterers justify your fact) if you transfer the glory of that honor in which you now stand to any other thing, then to the dispensation of His mercy which only makes that lawful to your grace which nature and law denies to all woman.

Neither would I that your grace should fear that this your humiliation before God should in any case infirm or weaken your just and lawful authority before men. Nay madam such unfeigned confession of God's benefits received shall be the establishment of the same, not only to yourself, but also to your seed and posterity. When contrariwise, a proud conceit and elevation of yourself shall be the occasion that your reign shall be unstable, troublesome, and short.

God is witness that unfeignedly, I both love and reverence your grace – yea, I pray that your reign may be long, prosperous, and quiet. And that for the quietness which Christ's members before persecuted have received under you.

But that if I should flatter Your Grace, I [would be] no friend, but [rather], a [deceitful] traitor. And therefore of conscience I am compelled to say, that neither the consent of people, the process of tyme, nor multitude of men, can establish a law which God shall approve; but whatsoever he approves (by his eternal Word), that shall be approved, and whatsoever he damns shall [be condemned], though all men in earth would hazard the justification of the same.

And therefore, Madam, the only way to retain and to keep those benefits of God abundantly poured now of late days upon you and your realm, is unfeignedly to render under God, to his mercy and undeserved grace the whole glory of this your exaltation, forget your birth and all titles which thereupon do hinge, and consider deeply how for fear of your life, ye did decline from **God**, and bow to idolatry. Let it not appear a small offense in your eyes, that you have declined from **Christ Jesus** in the day of his battle; neither yet would I that you should esteem that mercy to be vulgar and common which you have received.

To wit, that **God** has covered your former offense, has presented you when you were most unthankful, and in the end has exalted and raised you up not only from the dust, but also from the ports (gates) of death to rule above his people for the comfort of his kirk. It appertains to you therefore to ground the justice of your authority not upon that law which from year to year does change, but upon the eternal providence of him who contrary to nature, and without your deserving has thus exalted your head.

If thus in God's presence you humble yourself, as in my heart I glorify **God** for that rest granted to his afflicted flock within England under yow a weak instrument, so will I with tongue and pen justify your authority and regiment as the **Holy Ghost** has justified the same in **Deborah**, that blessed mother in Israel. But if these premises (as **God** forbid) [are] neglected, you shall begin to brag of your birth, and to build your authority upon your own law, flatter you who so list your felicity shall be short.

Interpret my rude words in the best part as written by him who is no enemy to your grace.

By diverse letters I have required license to visit your realm not to seek myself neither yet my own ease, or [convenience]. Which if you now refuse and. deny I must remit my [...] to **God**, adding this for conclusion: that commonly it is seen that such as love not the counsel of the faithful (appear it never so sharp) are compelled to follow the deceit of flatterers to their own perdition.

The mighty Spirit of the Lord Jesus move your heart to understand what is said, give unto you the discretion of spirits, and so rule you in all your actions and enterprises that in you **God** may be glorified, his church edified, and you yourself as a lively member of the same may be an example and mirror of virtue and of godly life unto others.

So be it. Of Edinburgh, July 20th, 1559
By your graces wholly to command in godliness.

Endorsed.
JOHN KNOX

To the right mighty, right high, and right excellent
Princess **Elizabeth**, Queen of England, etc.
Be these delivered State Papers, Scotland, Vol. 1 Art. 65.

---

20 MARCH 1561. THOMAS RANDOLPH to Sir WILLIAM CECIL. [From Berwick on Tweed.]

Master Knox in certain articles given unto my Lord James at this time has mitigated somewhat the rigor of his book, referring much unto the time that the same was written.

State Papers, Scotland, Vol. 6, Art. 37.

JOHN KNOX'S SECOND DEFENSE TO QUEEN ELIZABETH.
AUGUST 5TH, 1561

GRACE from GOD the Father through our Lord Jesus with perpetual increase of his Holy Spirit. May it please your majesty that it is here certainly spoken that the Queen of Scotland (Mary Queen of Scots) travails earnestly to have a treatise entitled *The First Blast of the Trumpet Confuted by the Answer of the Learned in Diverse Realms*. And further, that she labors to inflame the hearts of princes against the writer. And because that it may appear that your majesty has interest, that she minds to travail with Your Grace, Your Grace's counsel, and learned men for judgment against such a common enemy to women and to their regiment.

It [would be] but foolishness to me to prescribe unto Your Majesty what is to be done in anything but especially in such things as men suppose do touch myself. But of one thing I think myself assured, and therefore I dare not conceal it, to wit: that neither does our sovereign so greatly fear her own estate by reason of that book, neither yet does she so unfeignedly favor the tranquility of Your Majesty's reign and realm that she would tack so great and earnest pains [only] that her crafty counsel in so doing shot at a further mark.

Two years ago, I wrote unto Your Majesty my full declaration touching that work. Experience since has shown that I am not desirous of innovations (i.e. in government), so that **Christ Jesus** is not in his members openly trodden under the feet of the ungodly. With further purgation, I will not trouble Your Majesty for the present.

Beseeching the Eternal so to assist Your Highness in all affairs, that in his sight you may be found acceptable, your regiment profitable to your commonwealth, and your facts (deeds) to be such that justly they may be praised of all godly unto the coming of the Lord **Jesus**, to whose mighty protection I unfeignedly commit Your Majesty.

From Edinburgh, August 5th, 1561
Your Majesty's servant to command in godliness

Endorsed
JOHN KNOX

To the mighty and excellent princess **Elizabeth,** the Queen's Majesty of **England**, be these delivered.

State Papers, Scotland, Vol. 6, Art 55.

ESPITE this triumphant appeal to his quiet citizenship under **Mary Stuart**, the following description of her mother shows that the great Scotsman never altered his private opinion on this subject.

The peace as said is contracted. The queen dowager passed by sea to France with galleys that for that purpose were prepared and took with her diverse of the nobility of Scotland. The earls **Huntly, Glencairne, Mershell, Casilles**; the lords **Maxwell** flying, Sir **George Dowglasse**, together with all the king's sons, and diverse barons, and gentlemen of ecclesiastical estate; the Bishop of **Galloway**, and many others, with promise that they should be richly rewarded for their good service.

What they received, we cannot tell, but few were made rich at their returning. The dowager had to practice somewhat with her brethren, the Duke of **Gwyse** and the Cardinal of **Loraine**. The weight whereof, the governor after felt, for shortly after his returning, was the governor deposed of the government (justly by **God**, but most unjustly by man) and she made regent, in the year of our Lord 1554. And a crown put upon her head, as seemly a sight (if men had eyes) as to put a saddle upon the back of an unruly cow.

And so began she to practice, practice upon practise, how France might be advanced, hir friends made rich, and she brought to immortall glory. For that was her common talk: "So that I may procure the wealth and honor of my friends, and a good fame unto myself, I regard not what GOD do after with me."

And in very deed, in deep dissimulation to bring her own purpose to effect, she passed the common sort of women, as we will after hear. But yet **God**, to whose gospel she declared herself [an] enemy, in the end [did] frustrate her of her devices.

The History of the Church of Scotland, pp. 192-193.
(Ed. 1584)

www.ingramcontent.com/pod-product-compliance
Lightning Source LLC
Chambersburg PA
CBHW020243010526
44107CB00002B/75